Chipper Jones

A Brave Legend in the Making

BECKETT PUBLICATIONS
DALLAS, TEXAS

Book design by Sara Maneval.
Photo credits: p.128

Chipper Jones: A Brave Legend in the Making
Copyright ©2000 by Beckett Publications
All rights reserved under International and Pan-American Copyright Conventions.

Published by: Beckett Publications
15850 Dallas Parkway
Dallas, Texas 75248

ISBN: 1-887432-89-2
Beckett™ is a registered trademark of Beckett Publications.

First Edition: March 2000

Beckett Corporate Sales and Information (972) 991-6657

Contents

Hank Aaron, the career home run king, spent twenty-one of his twenty-three major-league seasons playing for the Braves. Now an executive with Atlanta, Aaron was named to baseball's Team of the Century in October 1999.

Foreword

BY HANK AARON
AS TOLD TO DAN SCHLOSSBERG

Chipper Jones has as much talent as anybody I've ever seen. If he keeps producing like he's been producing, I think he certainly can be a candidate for the Baseball Hall of Fame.

I think he could do a lot of things — five hundred home runs, MVP awards and more. He's beginning to have a lot of confidence in himself. I think he feels like he can walk up to the plate and get a base hit no matter who's out there pitching.

When a hitter feels that way and

Hank Aaron sees Chipper as a candidate for the Baseball Hall of Fame — if his offensive production stays where it has been the last several years.

has a little bit of ability — or especially someone with a lot of ability like Chipper — I think he can do a lot of good things. Right now I think Chipper is beginning to blossom into the kind of hitter we all thought he would probably be.

I played in Milwaukee with Eddie Mathews, another third baseman who hit a lot of home runs. In the sense of determination and wanting to win, I think Chipper and Eddie are probably about the same. But Chipper might be a better hitter because he's a switch-hitter. He can take away the advantage some of the hard-throwing lefthanders have by switching to the other side of the plate.

From what I gathered, Don Baylor [former Atlanta hitting coach] was very instrumental in helping Chipper develop more power from the right side. It seems to me that Don found something about Chipper that nobody else knew about.

He hit forty-five home runs in 1999 and could have broken my Atlanta club record of forty-seven — especially if he'd had Andres Galarraga [out for the year with cancer] batting behind him all season. There's no doubt in my mind that Chipper has a good shot at Mickey Mantle's record for home runs by a switch-hitter [fifty-four in 1961]. It's going to be tough but he certainly will have an opportunity to do it.

I was glad to see him get the National League's MVP award. There are several things that made him into the Most Valuable Player.

First of all, he had an outstanding year and probably carried the team on his own

"Chipper is a team player who leads by example," says Aaron.

Jones is a strong candidate to join Hank Aaron and Dale Murphy as the only Braves to produce thirty home run – thirty stolen base seasons.

"If the Braves can come up with somebody at third base, you could easily find Chipper Jones in the outfield," says Aaron. "There I think you're going to really see him blossom into the kind of hitter I think he probably could be."

Both Aaron
and Jones have
National
League MVP
awards to their
credit —
Aaron in 1957
and Chipper
in 1999.

shoulders for the last month or so. He did all the little things: hitting for average, hitting for power and getting on base with a lot of walks.

I think that's what an MVP award means. If a player can carry a team on his shoulders and somehow win a few more ballgames than somebody else could.

Dale Murphy won back-to-back MVP awards with the Braves [in 1982–83] but Chipper's a better hitter, average-wise. Like Chipper, Dale had the desire and determination to win and excel.

everything came together for Chipper during the two series we played against the Mets in the last two weeks of September in 1999. Chipper had a tremendous two weeks but they just kept pitching to him. They kept pitching and pitching and he kept hitting and hitting. And all the hits he got were big hits: He hit the ball out of the ballpark, got doubles and triples and things like that. He was a one-man gang, really, in more ways than one. And we won five of those six games.

I was amazed the Mets kept pitching to him; I think the Astros and Yankees wised up a little bit in the postseason, though he did hit a home run in the World Series.

People ask me if Chipper's performance reminded me of the home run I hit off Billy Muffett of the Cardinals in 1957 to win the 1957 National League pennant for the Milwaukee Braves. The answer is no: That was just one home run. Chipper was hot for a couple of weeks.

It was obvious that Chipper was immune to pressure. I thought he handled the pressure situations well. The comments he made about Mets fans [when he told them to go home and put on their Yankee hats] were no big deal. Whatever was said was said in innocence. He wasn't saying anything to be harsh or nasty. All of that was blown out of proportion by the media. Chipper's not the kind of person to go out and talk like that.

In fact, Chipper is a team player who leads by example. He signed as a short-stop and can play almost any position. I know how important it is to be versa-tile: although I spent most of my career in right field, I was a second baseman in the minors and also played first, second, third, left field and center for the Braves. I was a designated hitter for the Milwaukee Brewers, who were then in the American League, my last two years.

He had an outstanding year at third base but I think if he goes to the outfield you may see him hit fifty home runs. You may see him hit .330. You may see him score some runs. You may even see him steal a bunch of bases. If he goes to the out-field, it's going to take a lot of pressure off him that exists now because he plays third base.

Chipper Jones is a franchise player — very much so. He's very important to the Braves. Without him, I don't think the Braves would have won anything the last few years.

If I were starting a team, he'd be one of the first players I'd consider. There are some other great players out there too but you would certainly have to look at somebody like Chipper Jones. His credentials speak for themselves.

Hank Aaron says that Chipper may score more runs and steal more bases if he's moved from third base to the outfield because he'll be able to focus on his offense.

Drafted directly from high school, Chipper wasn't done growing. Now 6-foot-4, he has added a significant amount of muscle to his frame. His growth made the move from shortstop to third base logical.

employee
No.10

BY BOBBY COX
AS TOLD TO DAN SCHLOSSBERG

After scouting Chipper Jones at The Bolles High School in Jacksonville, Florida, Bobby Cox knew he was on to something. "He was a shortstop then and a pretty good one," says Cox. "He had good hands, ran good and looked like a heck of a hitter."

I first became aware of Chipper Jones when I was general manager of the Braves.

We had the first pick in the draft that year [1990] and he was at the top of our list — along with a couple of other guys.

It's a funny thing trying to see a real good ballplayer like that. It's hard sometimes because other teams don't pitch to him. That time of year in the spring, there's a lot of rain in Florida too. I had [current Boston manager] Jimy Williams see him and [former farm director] Paul Snyder saw him a lot and loved him. Other guys did too.

Chipper was a pretty impressive kid. If you walked into a high school ballpark and told your scouts, "Don't tell me which guy you're going to look at," even before he stepped out onto the field, you'd point at Chipper and say, "That's the guy we came to look at." Chipper Jones looked like a ballplayer.

He was a shortstop then and a pretty good one. He had

good hands, ran good and looked like a heck of a hitter. I didn't even know he switch-hit until I saw him for the second time. I thought he was just a right-handed hitter.

But one time during spring training Jimy Williams wanted to see his daughter swim in a tournament up near where Chipper was going to school. I said, "Okay, you can go see your daughter swim as long as you stop by and see Chipper play in a ballgame." Jimy saw him hit a home run left-handed that night so that was good news.

Chipper is a student of the game. From the dugout he always watches pitchers and stays keenly aware of the game situation.

I don't think I ever would have projected him to become a forty-five-home run man. But you never know: A lot of guys, including Brooks Robinson and Alan Trammell, didn't hit more than four or five in their first couple of years. It's hard to judge sometimes. Swings change, kids get stronger, and this and that.

I always thought Chipper had "All-Star" written on him. I didn't know what his numbers would be, but he did have that All-Star look about him.

The only thing we weren't sure about was his position. He's a big kid — 6'3" or 6'4" and 220 pounds. We were

"It looks like he has a lot of fun playing the game," says Darrell Evans former Braves third baseman. "He's the kind of guy everybody looks to as a leader."

Bobby Cox was the general manager of the Braves when they drafted Chipper Jones. A few months later he became manager and helped lead the Braves to five World Series appearances in the '90s.

"I always thought Chipper had 'All-Star' written on him," says Cox. "I didn't know what his numbers would be, but he did have that All-Star look about him."

MAJOR LEAGUE BASEBALL AMATEUR DRAFT
All-Time No. 1 Picks

1999	Josh Hamilton	of	Tampa Bay
1998	Pat Burrell	inf	Philadelphia
1997	Matt Anderson	p	Detroit
1996	Kris Benson	p	Pittsburgh
1995	Darin Erstad	of-p	California
1994	Paul Wilson	p	New York Mets
1993	Alex Rodriguez	ss	Seattle
1992	Phil Nevin	3b	Houston
1991	Brien Taylor	p	New York Yankees
1990	Chipper Jones	ss	Atlanta
1989	Ben McDonald	p	Baltimore
1988	Andy Benes	p	San Diego
1987	Ken Griffey Jr.	of	Seattle
1986	Jeff King	inf	Pittsburgh
1985	B.J. Surhoff	c	Milwaukee
1984	Shawn Abner	of	New York Mets
1983	Tim Belcher	p	Minnesota
1982	Shawon Dunston	ss	Chicago Cubs
1981	Mike Moore	p	Seattle
1980	Darryl Strawberry	of	New York Mets
1979	Al Chambers	of	Seattle
1978	Bob Horner	3b	Atlanta
1977	Harold Baines	of	Chicago White Sox
1976	Floyd Bannister	p	Houston
1975	Danny Goodwin	c	California
1974	Bill Almon	inf	San Diego
1973	David Clyde	p	Texas
1972	Dave Roberts	inf	San Diego
1971	Danny Goodwin	c	Chicago White Sox
1970	Mike Ivie	c	San Diego
1969	Jeff Burroughs	of	Washington
1968	Tim Foli	inf	New York Mets
1967	Ron Blomberg	1b	New York Yankees
1966	Steve Chilcott	c	New York Mets
1965	Rick Monday	c	Kansas City Athletics

going to let him play himself off short for sure. I'm not so sure he still couldn't play shortstop to some degree and play it pretty well. But he's become one of the premier defensive third basemen so I think we made the right choice [moving him there in 1995] and so does he.

I think Chipper's defensive skills are good right now. There's a lot of action at third base, of course, and you're in every play. Maybe he'd have more time to think about hitting if he were an outfielder — I don't know — but I think Chipper prefers to play where the action is.

I think it's a little easier to play the outfield than the infield positions. But

Chipper's power production jumped when batting right-handed in 1999. He went from hitting only two homers off left-handed pitching in 1998 to fifteen in 1999.

you don't know if he'd be out there thinking too much or if playing there would conserve his strength and make him stronger at the plate.

Chipper could play center field if he wanted to; he'd be an excellent center fielder. He's one of those gifted guys who could play any position and look good doing it.

He's certainly one of the top fifteen players in the game. He can steal a base, play defense, hit home runs, hit for average and even bunt a ball if he wants to. Chipper Jones can do a lot of things. He's got great power from both sides of the dish. I think he compares favorably to any star you can name.

Don Baylor did a super job with Chipper last year. His home run production from the right side really perked up. He hit .300 as a right-handed batter the year before too but didn't hit many home runs. They worked on that part of it and it really paid off.

"Every once in awhile, a player with the looks of a Dale Murphy or a Chipper Jones comes up and gets the fans excited," says Cox. "They become the big star, the franchise player, for your team or your town. Dale and Chipper both have that All-American type of appearance and image."

Chipper really turned it on when we needed him. He got awfully hot with the lumber — it reminded me of the way Fred McGriff carried us down the stretch in 1993. Last year, it seemed like Chipper was getting every big hit during the ballgame.

When you're going down the stretch and you've got a good ball club, you need for somebody to get hot. Last year, it was Chipper Jones.

He had that one-game lead over the Mets with two weeks left, but had to play them in two three-game series, home and away. We were looking to score a run any way we could, to jump out in front, just to win the series. We were just hoping for somebody to get hot and also hoping that nobody cooled off. Chipper came through for us and helped himself become the Most Valuable Player in the National League.

I think MVPs are clutch players. Certainly he is a real clutch player for us.

he works awfully hard on his game. Chipper studies the game all the time. And he studies hard. He's quiet once in awhile because he's watching — he's watching the pitchers, he's watching a lot of things. He has become more of a team leader, I think, and I'm sure he'll be more of one in the future. He's a guy who can lead anything.

There's a definite parallel between Chipper and Dale Murphy, who came up during my first stint as manager of the Braves and later won back-to-back MVP awards.

Every once in awhile, a player with the looks of a Dale Murphy or a Chipper Jones comes up and gets the fans excited. They become the big star, the franchise player, for your team or your town. Dale and Chipper both have that All-American type of appearance and image.

Like Dale, Chipper is going to be a perennial All-Star. He's always going to have big numbers up there. I foresee a smooth and consistent career. I don't see a lot of peaks and valleys.

Chipper is going to have a great career. I just hope it's always with the Braves.

"I think MVPs are clutch players,"
says Bobby Cox. "Certainly he is
a real clutch player for us."

CHAPTER 2

Heart
of the Braves

I BY MARTY NOBLE

the last of four crushing home runs, four magnificent Chip Shots, was sailing to an area well beyond the reach of any Mets outfielder, putting the Braves well beyond the reach of any Mets hope for a first-place finish. Chipper Jones had struck again, and the Mets had been struck down, yet again. "Chip-wrecked" a New York tabloid would say.

Jones had hit two home runs in the Braves 2–1 victory against their closest pursuer. He had hit another and driven in two more runs in the first inning the next night, sending an unmistakable message to the Mets — "This is not the year you catch us." And finally on the next afternoon after the Mets had conceded they probably should have pitched around him, he hit another home run, this one with two runners

In a late 1999 September series, Chipper Jones nearly single-handedly dismantled the Mets with four home runs and seven RBIs. The series sweep secured Atlanta's lead in the NL East.

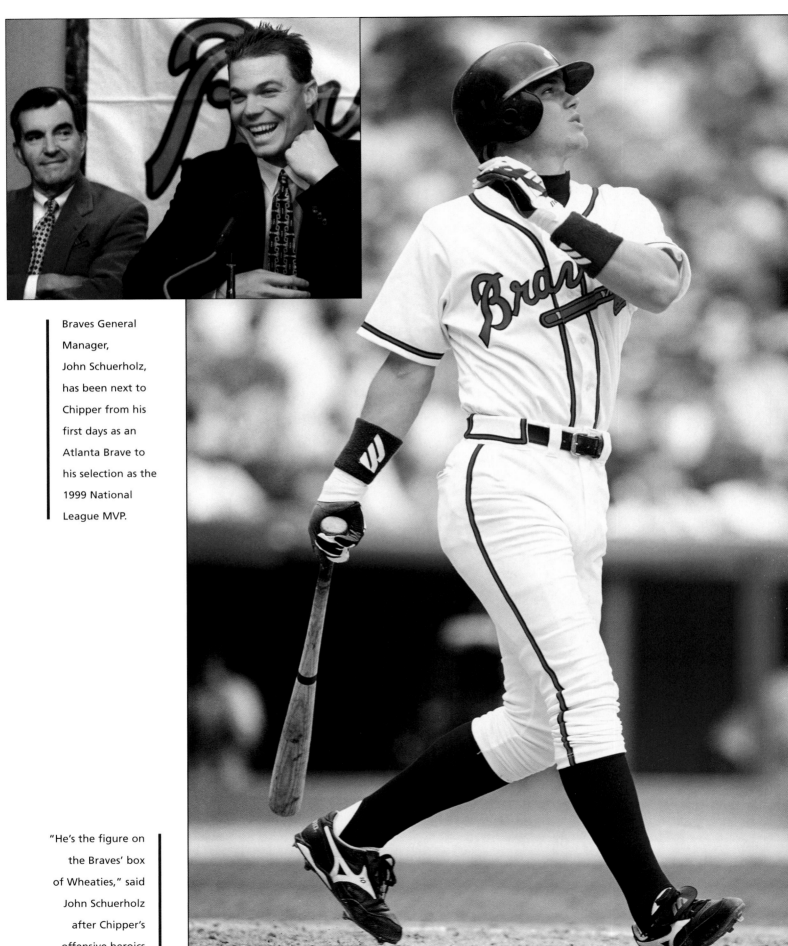

Braves General Manager, John Schuerholz, has been next to Chipper from his first days as an Atlanta Brave to his selection as the 1999 National League MVP.

"He's the figure on the Braves' box of Wheaties," said John Schuerholz after Chipper's offensive heroics against the Mets.

on base, this one the telling blow in a four-run rally that all but secured a 6–3 victory. A sweet September series sweep in 1999 of the team the Braves love to beat.

In one brief late-summer sequence, Jones had transformed the Chop Shop into the Chip Shop, the National League East race into a process of elimination and himself into the prohibitive favorite for the National League Most Valuable Player Award.

Braves general manager John Schuerholz took in and processed all that had occurred in twenty-seven innings, concluding that the Braves had put enough daylight between themselves and the Mets so that an eighth successive division championship was in the offing. And that his third baseman had moved well ahead of the MVP field as well. And at the same time, Schuerholz couldn't help but develop a sense of deja vu. He had seen this show — a third baseman in his command pummels a New York team in critical, late-season games.

In three games in the third week of September, Jones had been to the Mets what George Brett had been to the Yankees in four October playoff series beginning in 1976 and running through 1980: public enemy No. 1. When Jones had completed his destruction of the Mets, Schuerholz figured he had watched a sequel.

Chipper and Brett, Brett and Chipper; the parallels were there to be seen, there to be identified by the man with a unique perspective. Schuerholz had identified the parallels long before Jones took Rick Reed deep in the first inning of the first Mets-Braves engagement September 21. "Both play third, both bat third," he said.

And as the Braves series unfolded and Jones unloaded, the similarities were reinforced. The Mets didn't have a pitch, a pitcher or even a notion of how to get Chipper out. And that's how it had been with Brett and the Yankees back then, the overriding differences being that Jones' dominance was contained in three Braves victories while Brett's lasted from year to year and the Yankees prevailed three times in four series despite his exploits.

"It was a lot like George and the Yankees," Schuerholz said. "No matter what they tried, George was right on the pitch. And it was that way every time we played the Yankees. I've often thought about how similar Chipper is to George in a lot of ways. And that series [against the Mets] brought it all back."

Schuerholz was a rising executive with the Royals in the Seventies when the team won four division championships in a five-year sequence with Brett serving as centerpiece of the batting order. And he has been the Braves general manager since October, 1990, the last October in which the Braves didn't play baseball.

The Braves, under then-general manager Bobby Cox, had made Jones the first player selected in the amateur draft some four months before Schuerholz' arrival. Schuerholz was there to witness Jones' evolution as he had been there in Kansas City, monitoring the prenatal stage of what became Brett's Hall of Fame career.

"It's been a privilege to watch each," he says.

The Braves could have missed on Jones. They could have spent the first selection in the 1990 draft on Todd Van Poppel, the Texas schoolboy sensation who eventually emerged as the fourteenth player selected by the Athletics, and

Schuerholz sees a resemblance between George Brett and Chipper. "Both play third, both bat third," says Schuerholz. "I've often thought about how similar Chipper is to George in a lot of ways."

Bobby Cox had the opportunity to choose Todd Van Poppel with the number one pick in the 1990 draft but went with Chipper Jones — a decision that is still paying off.

who, by letter, had warned clubs against choosing him because of an intention to attend college.

But the pitcher's announced intent changed nothing for the Braves. Cox and Paul Snyder, then the assistant vice-president for scouting, had seen a switch-hitting shortstop from Jacksonville, Florida who had speed and power and, as Cox later told Schuerholz, "a special look in his eyes."

"I heard a lot about that look," Schuerholz said. "Bobby was very taken by Chipper . . . the letter of admonition be damned."

Schuerholz soon saw the look for himself, liked what saw and likened it to what Frank Cashen, one of his mentors with the Orioles in the Sixties, identified as "fire in the belly." Chipper was ablaze inside.

"The first time you saw him, you had an idea he was special. The second time, you were sure of it," Cox said. "You could make a quick observation with him because he was so talented. But no one wanted to be quick in and quick out. You wanted to stick around and watch."

"Provided he stayed healthy, there was no reason to doubt he would develop into one of the elite players," Schuerholz said.

Then Jones tore apart his knee in spring training, 1994 with his general manager in attendance. "My first reaction was, 'This is a baseball tragedy,'" Schuerholz said. "This was a potential cornerstone player." But a knee injury could compromise every phase of Jones' games.

"Quickness and reflexes are essentials for shortstops. With a major knee injury [a rupture of the anterior cruciate ligament], you had to wonder whether he would be diminished," Schuerholz said.

But as he monitored Jones' reha-
bilitation from reconstructive surgery,
his saw that look on a regular basis.
The injury would be a detour, but
hardly a roadblock. "The vigor he
showed in rehabbing convinced me
he'd be back," the general manager
said. "The skill of the surgeon and
Chipper's vigorous rehab made him
whole again." And Jones became an
elite player as Schuerholz had antici-
pated, a Most Valuable Player.

Within months of Brett's induction into The Baseball Hall of
Fame and nineteen years after Brett was elected American League MVP, Jones
was the near-unanimous choice of the Baseball Writers Association for the
National League award. Another parallel for Schuerholz to consider.

Both Schuerholz
and Cox liked
what they saw in
Chipper very early.
Cox spotted "a
special look in his
eyes" before
drafting Jones.

"Each has been a key member of his team's offense," the general manager
said. "Significant middle-of-the-lineup guys. But I think in George's case, his
team's relied on him more than our [Braves] teams have relied on Chipper."

Then other injuries changed them too. The Braves began the 1999 season
without Andres Galarraga, and lost Javy Lopez by early summer. When Brian
Jordan's offense was compromised by a hand injury, Jones essentially stood
alone and unprotected in the Braves batting order, and the Braves stood —
barely. Even the vaunted pitching wasn't what it had been.

But just when they seemed most vulnerable, Jones seemed most valuable.
The Mets invaded Atlanta, trailing the Braves by a game and intent on leaving
with at least a share of the division lead. Then Chipper flexed, resulting in four

In 1999 Chipper averaged a home run every 12.6 at-bats — the same ratio as Ken Griffey Jr.

In his 1995 rookie
season, Chipper
had some prob-
lems defensively
with twenty-five
errors at third
base. His error
total has never
been that high
since, and he had
a career low of
twelve errors in
1998.

home runs and seven RBI in three games and underscoring Schuerholz' sense of his identity. "He's the figure on the Braves' box of Wheaties," the general manager said.

Even with all those Cy Young Award winners, even with Galarraga and Lopez to share the crowded spotlight, even with the turmoil in Jones' personal life — a divorce and his candid public mea culpas. "Chipper is the unquestioned darling of our team, just like George was in Kansas City," Schuerholz says.

Chipper completely tore his ACL during spring training in 1994. After missing a year to rehab his knee, Chipper came back with a vengeance in '95 and was named The Sporting News Rookie of the Year (voted on by the players).

Jones could be compared with worse. "It's inescapable for me," Schuerholz says. "Of course there are differences. And there is one area in which I wish Chipper was a lot more like George. I don't see in Chipper the unbounded joy that I saw every day in George. Chipper and I have talked about it. You should enjoy being able to play at that level. George showed it in practice — anytime he was on the field.

"I don't see it so often in Chipper. It might just be part of the maturing process. And I think when it comes, he'll be a better player because of it."

CHAPTER 3

Chip
off the old block

BY LARRY JONES SR.
AS TOLD TO DAN SCHLOSSBERG

Chipper used a strike zone painted on the back of the wooden garage at the horse farm where his mom, Lynne Jones, an accomplished equestrienne, teaches dressage. Dad, Larry Sr., would stand in front of the barn and pitch tennis balls to Chipper.

Chipper showed his first interest in baseball when he was about three years old. I was a high school coach and every day when we practiced, he wanted to come to the field.

Kids being kids, they aren't going to sit around in the stands. If the ball's rolling, they're going to run out there and pick it up. My high school kids played with him a little bit. We'd stick a bat in his hands and try to underhand the ball to him. It kind of went from there.

He started in what we call a minor league. He pitched and played shortstop. I don't remember him playing any other position. But when he got to the American Legion team in DeLand, they had a pretty good shortstop so they played Chipper in right field a little bit.

He was a pretty good pitcher. He threw the ball in the mid-to-high 80s and had a little bit of a breaking ball. When he was a junior, he won all five of the games through the state championship game.

he became a switch-hitter on his own. We'd watch the old Game of the Week on Saturday afternoons. Then we'd go outside and imitate the game. If a left-handed hitter came up, you'd have to hit left-handed. I remember Chipper imitating Reggie Smith, the old switch-hitter for the Dodgers. He'd imitate his various stances — I used to laugh at him like crazy. It got to the point where Chipper was a pretty good left-handed hitter.

When I sent him to baseball school with Pete Dunn, our head coach at Stetson, Pete wrote on his evaluation that he had a better swing left-handed than he had right-handed — even though he was a natural right-handed batter.

Chipper perfected his swing playing Little League in Pierson, Florida.

This is one thing he and I have talked about ever since he's been a pro: You're going to get 400-450 at-bats left-handed every year and 150-160 at-bats right-handed. In order for you to keep the right-handed side sharp, you've got to work on it a little more than you do your left-handed side. I'm not real sure Chipper did that up until Don Baylor made him do it last season.

I'll never forget this: When Chipper was working out with us at Stetson last spring, he went down to Disney and had a hitting session two days before

Larry Jones Sr. grew up in Vero Beach, the home of Dodgertown, and was an avid Dodger fan. That may be why a young Chipper Jones is wearing a Dodgers batting helmet in this snapshot.

While in eighth grade Chipper played for the DeLand Babe Ruth All-Stars.

Chip off the old block? Larry Sr. played college baseball at Stetson University. "I was a shortstop too, back in the days when college players hit with wood bats," says Larry Sr.

spring training. He came back here and the door hadn't even slammed shut yet when he said, "Dad, the worm has turned around here."

He went into the little spiel about Don asking him what his philosophy was and he said, "I want to hit line drives, I want to drive in runs, I want to put together a good at-bat." Don said, "Bullshit." He said, "You hit third for one of the best teams in baseball and you're going to put fear into a manager's mind when he turns you around."

Chipper said his left-handed batting-practice pitcher didn't show up that day, so he put his bats back into his bag and was getting ready to leave after hitting left-handed. Don told him to bring his $4 million dollar ass back into the cage — he wasn't leaving until he hit right-handed.

Chipper needed somebody like that, somebody who wasn't intimidated by him. He needed someone to say, "This is the way you're going to do it. This is the way I operate." And for Chipper to have enough respect for that person to say "OK."

For that, I thank Don Baylor. I told his wife in the stands one time during the season that he's the best thing that ever happened to my son.

I think [new hitting coach] Merv Rettenmund is going to help him too. I really enjoyed listening to him during the Championship Series the Braves played against the San Diego Padres in 1998. Ken Caminiti came up and he said, "He's going to work you away, so just take the ball right back up the middle." And sure enough, he hammered it right back up the middle for a hit that drove in two runs. I like that philosophy.

I never coached Chipper formally. I believe that dads should not be on the competitive field with their sons.

I was coaching at Taylor High School when Chipper was getting ready to go out for the varsity team. I went to my boss and said I'm a big believer in not coaching my own son. I didn't want to put too much pressure on him and didn't want people to think I catered to him.

Chipper went to Bolles, a boarding school, after his freshman year at Taylor. He was catching some breaks at Taylor — I don't know whether it was because I worked at the school — and was bringing home As and Bs even though I never saw him bring home a book. I didn't like that so Lynne and I decided we'd send him up to Bolles to board during the week and bring him home on the weekends.

It was a little bit of a culture shock for him. He had some friends who went there, including one of the football players. He went pretty easily but I do know that he called home every day the first six weeks and said, "Dad, I'll never be eligible to play because I got blue-slipped by six of my teachers."

Chipper played basketball and football in high school. He liked the pressure of shooting the game-deciding free throws for the Pierson Taylor basketball team.

The Bolles School, the Jacksonville private school where Chipper was sent as a high school sophomore, retired Chipper's uniform No. 10. Chipper wore that number because his father also wore No. 10 when he played.

I told him I believed that if you let kids quit once, it would be easier to quit the second time. I told him, "Coming home is not an option."

We agreed that at the end of the school year, if he really tried and couldn't make it, we'd think about it. At the end of the first nine weeks, his grade-point average was 3.2 [out of a 4.0 maximum] and I never got another call about not having enough time or the work being too hard.

I really believe kids will give you what you demand of them, not what you ask of them. He decided, "Hey, if I don't get off the stick, I'm not going to be able to play." All of a sudden, things started falling into place.

In addition to high school ball, Chipper played in Little League, Babe Ruth

Larry Sr. says that Chipper needed someone such as Don Baylor (former Braves hitting coach), who's not intimidated by him, to help him improve batting right-handed.

League and American Legion ball. But I stuck to my guns and never coached him officially. When we worked out on our own, I was a fundamentals guy when we hit and when we took groundballs or worked on other things.

I thought he was a pretty coachable kid. But Chipper is the kind of guy who you cannot tell things to. He's got to see them; he's a mimicker.

Every now and then, he'll call when he's going through a hard time and I'll try to tell him some things. But it doesn't seem to work unless I can find it on a tape I've got of him. I'll send him the tape with a note that says, "Look at this particular at-bat and what's going on — that's what it looks like to me right now." Then I'll show him another tape with a note that says, "This is what you need to look like."

I don't know if you ever know for sure that a kid is going to become a big star — let alone make the major leagues. I can remember when Chipper was a twelve-year-old Little Leaguer. There was a team from Altamont Springs that had Jason Varitek and a couple of other kids who went to the finals of the Little League World Series. They had to beat Chipper's team to get out of their district.

It was a tie game, Chipper hit a home run, and then they tied it up again. It went into extra innings. It ended with Chipper hitting three home runs and winning the game. On the way home, I told my wife that I thought Chipper might be one of the ten best players of his age in the country. She said, "Yeah, right, you're a Little League dad."

I don't let her forget that. Every time he wins an award or something, I always say, "See? I told you."

I have seen so many good players never make it. I don't think you really, really know until they get there and — this is the important thing — they continue to improve after they get there. Somebody asked me the difference between the guys who make the big leagues and the guys who excel in the big leagues.

Chipper was a terror on the mound in high school. As a junior at The Bolles High School, he won all five of the team's playoff games through the state championship.

I go back to Michael Jordan. He was a great player in college. He was a first-round draft pick. But he refused to be a mediocre player.

After winning
the state cham-
pionship, Chipper
first went to his
father for a hug.

Chipper and his father didn't spend much time in the dugout together. Larry Sr. was a big believer in not managing his own son. "I didn't want to put too much pressure on him and didn't want people to think I catered to him," says Larry Sr.

The Chicago Bulls won their first championship and he could have rested on his laurels. They won their second championship and he could have rested on his laurels. Instead, he continued to improve.

I think there is something within a great player that refuses to accept mediocrity. I don't know what that is — I could make a bunch of money if I knew it — but there's something within a kid or a player's makeup that will not allow him to just be mediocre and just be there.

Chipper is much more of a student of the game now than he used to be. He was always the kind of kid who went out there and just did his thing. He wouldn't take the time to understand certain situations — what people were trying to do to him or the team. Over the years, since he's been a pro, he's become a real student of the game.

Larry Jones Sr. is assistant baseball coach at Stetson University in DeLand, Florida and an algebra teacher at Taylor High School in nearby Pierson.

Larry Jones Sr. and Lynne Jones make their home in Pierson, Florida.

He was sitting on our bench at Stetson on opening day a couple of years ago and was calling a squeeze play two hitters before it happened. I thought to myself at the time, "This is a kid who really thinks the game now." He didn't used to be like that.

As a player, that is the thing I am most struck with.

Of course, I never thought he would hit forty-five home runs either. I did think Chipper would be a .300 hitter in the big leagues. I thought he was a fifteen-to-twenty guy who might hit twenty-five in a really great year. But he developed a swing that generates some pop. When we were teaching him, it was "short stroke, stay behind the ball, don't go out and get it." He's lengthened his swing a little bit and I think it's generated some pop. Plus the fact he's a much bigger kid than he was then.

I heard Hank Aaron say he might hit sixty if he played the outfield. I do know this about the game: Infielders and the amount of play they get and the pressure that's on them is a whole lot more than outfielders face. When the Braves were talking about moving Chipper back to shortstop a couple of years ago, my good friend Tim Foli [a former major-league infielder] said it would be the worst thing that could ever happen to him offensively. He said Chipper would not be a consistent .300 hitter in the big leagues if he played shortstop.

What he was trying to say is that catching and the middle infield positions are so tough on you from a mental point of view that sometimes it hurts you at the plate.

I hate to mess with success. I believe if it ain't broke, don't try to fix it. I kind of like the idea that Chipper is an infielder in the big leagues — and a decent infielder in the big leagues. Do I think he could do better? Who knows?

The guys in the clubhouse call him Larry. They never call him Chipper. When we went to play golf with Greg Maddux at the Players Choice awards, we got to the first tee and Greg said, "Isn't this a bitch? What am I going to call both of you now?" Chipper said, "Call me Chipper. This is Larry."

Chipper and Larry Sr. have always enjoyed fishing and hunting together — Chipper still lists those as his hobbies in the Atlanta Braves media guide.

flipping the **Switch**

BY TONY GWYNN
AS TOLD TO BOB NIGHTENGALE

Tony Gwynn has been named to the All-Star Game fifteen times in his sixteen-year career with the San Diego Padres.

"In 1999, he just busted out," says Gwynn of Chipper's offensive outburst. "He stepped up and got up there with the Griffeys of the world, and did it all year long."

Chipper is one of my favorite players in the game.

You could see that he was going to be a great player when he came up, but the more you see him, the more you realize what a great future he has.

He's always been so mature. It's like he always had a game plan. He's a heady type of ballplayer. The instincts seem so natural to him. He plays the game the right way, and rarely will you ever see him make a mental mistake. Really, he's the complete package. He could play in any era and still fit in.

He's a guy who you would never question his heart and desire. He's always been a solid player, but now he's a great player. He wants to continue to improve, and will improve. It's hard to say after having a year like he did, he'll get better. But I think he will.

What made him so impressive this past year was the adjustments he made at the plate. Chipper made so many

Chipper has been named to the All-Star team three times in his career. He wasn't named to the team in 1999, but did manage to win the 1999 National League MVP award.

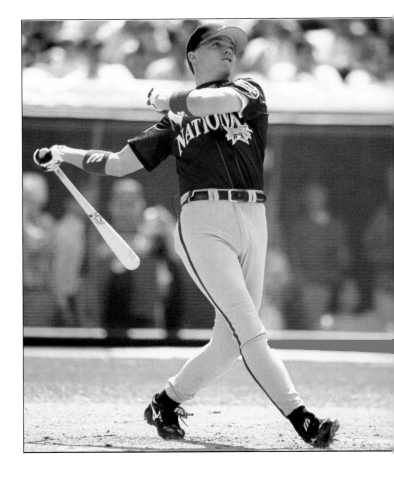

The winner of a National League record-tying eight batting titles, Tony Gwynn is regarded as one of the greatest pure hitters in baseball history. He is the league's active career batting leader (.339 average) and active hits leader (3,067 hits).

Gwynn sees Chipper as a player
who could play and fit in, in
any era of baseball.

Gwynn was impressed that Chipper had an approach to hitting, even early in his career.

adjustments to his right-handed swing. He's better right-handed now than ever before in his life. And you know what? He's only going to get better. It's scary knowing that he's going to even be better than he is now.

the thing that made him so dangerous was that he became a complete switch-hitter. He used to be so much better left-handed, but he made so many improvements right-handed, you can hardly tell the difference anymore.

He's always been a great hitter from the left side. He used to always hit to

all fields, and hit to all fields with power. That's what made him so good. But right-handed, he used to always be a dead-pull hitter, and without the power. He was much easier to defense batting right-handed. Now, he made himself consistently good both ways. He's got the same swing working both sides of the plate. That was never the case before.

We talk a lot when we see each other, and listening to him, he gives a lot of credit to Don Baylor, who was his hitting coach before leaving for the Cubs. What Don made him do was not to be afraid hitting the other way, right-handed. And look what happened. He stepped it up and became the MVP, like he should have. He did everything you had to do.

I know there's a lot of talk about what happens to Chipper now that Baylor has left for the Cubs. But to me, he's going to get even better, particularly with Merv Rettenmund becoming the Braves' hitting coach. I'm a big Merv Rettenmund fan. Merv is the best. You watch, Chipper's going to refine that stroke even more, and put up even bigger power numbers while hitting even more to all fields.

I know I wouldn't want to be a pitcher. How do you pitch to Chipper? You really can't. He has the ability to go the other way, and he does it like the big boys do it — goes the other way with authority. Come on, how do you pitch to a guy like that? I can tell you that no one thinks of Chipper as a straight pull-hitter now.

"He plays the game the right way, and rarely will you ever see him make a mental mistake," Gwynn says.

He's got the perfect make-up, too. He's never too high, never too low. He's pretty composed. And he's a leader. I can't see Atlanta ever letting him go. This guy should be with them for his entire career because he can do it all.

You talk about a complete player. What can't he do? He runs well, steals bases and is a solid defensive third baseman. But the thing that strikes me about him most is his willingness to learn.

I remember a couple of years ago, at his first All-Star Game, I asked him about his hitting style and what he was trying to do. He told me, "Left-handed, there's no question. I'm just trying to be aggressive and hit to all fields."' I asked, "OK, how about right-handed?" He said, "Right-handed, I'm just

"It's a lot of fun to watch that guy play," says Braves closer John Rocker. "He's one of the most talented ballplayers I've ever seen."

"You talk about a complete player," says Gwynn. "What can't he do? He runs well, steals bases and is a solid defensive third baseman."

CHIPPER JONES
CAREER BASERUNNING

Year	Team	Stolen Bases	Caught Stealing	Stolen Base Percentage	Grounded Into Double Play
1993	ATL	0	0	.00	0
1995	ATL	8	4	.67	10
1996	ATL	14	1	.93	14
1997	ATL	20	5	.80	19
1998	ATL	16	6	.73	17
1999	ATL	25	3	.89	20
TOTALS		83	19	.81	80

trying to get my hits, but not so much with power. I've got more pop left-handed."

He used a thirty-six-ounce bat left-handed and a thirty-four-ounce bat right-handed.

That impressed me that he had an approach from the get-go. It gives you an indication of what kind of player he is. He was already a good player, but he wanted to be a great player, and wasn't sure how to go about doing that.

Well, he sure answered that. In 1999, he just busted out. He stepped up and got up there with the Griffeys of the world, and did it all year long. It will be interesting to see what he can do to maintain this level. But now that he's there, you know what?

I think he'll be there for the next ten years. That's how much I believe in Chipper Jones.

"I know I wouldn't want to be a pitcher," says Gwynn. "How did you pitch to Chipper? You really can't."

A thirteen-time All-Star, George Brett entered the Baseball Hall of Fame in 1999. He won his third batting title in 1990 becoming the first player to win batting titles in three different decades.

CHAPTER 5

Fire
cool under

BY GEORGE BRETT
AS TOLD TO TRACY RINGOLSBY

i've developed an apprecia-
tion for Chipper Jones from afar. I
first got a chance to meet him in 1996
when I went to St. Louis during the
National League Championship Series.

I was there during the Braves' batting practice with John Schuerholz, the
Braves general manager. I've known
John since I signed with the Royals; he
was in the Royals front office at the
time. John and I were talking near the
batting cage and Chipper was hitting.
When Chipper came out of the cage,
John said, "Come here, I want you to
meet someone special."

I shook hands with Chipper and
told him good luck. Not that he
needed luck. He had that special aura.

You could tell by looking in his eyes that he was a determined player. You could see the fire in his eye. You have to admire that in a player.

It's like what Royals manager Tony Muser says about taking a pitcher out of the game. He goes to the mound and looks in their eyes. Sometimes he sees the back of their head. That's not good. Sometimes he can see the determination in a guy's eyes. Then you know they want the challenge. It's not that you can always meet the challenge, but at least you want it.

a nd Chipper wants that challenge.

Some people just want to be there when the pressure is on. And some guys, when it's a critical point in the game say to themselves, "I wish somebody else were up here instead of me."

With Chipper he looks at the challenge and says, "I want to be the guy up there."

As a player, I always wanted be the guy that if it came down to one at-bat, I wanted it on my shoulders to win or lose. I wasn't worried about being the goat. I'd go up there thinking, "Put the winning run on third in the ninth inning and I'll get him in." I always had that confidence in myself, like Chipper does. You don't always do it, but you have to feel you can.

You know there are going to be days when you have to deal with the media and explain why you didn't come through. But you also know the next day that chance could be there again and you can come through. You have to want to be in that situation to have a chance to succeed, and Chipper does. Once you

"You could tell by looking in his eyes that he was a determined player. You could see the fire in his eye," says George Brett after meeting Chipper Jones.

George Brett, a gold glover at third base, likes what he sees in Chipper's range and arm strength.

With the game on the line, Brett says he always wanted to be the one at bat and that Chipper is the same way.

wish someone else was up — you are going to make an out. You've buried yourself before you get to the plate.

It's like that old Pedro Guerrero reaction when he was with the Dodgers and their manager, Tommy Lasorda, asked, "What's your first thought when the game is on the line and we're in the field?" Pedro said, "Don't hit it to Steve Sax." So Lasorda asked him, "What's your second thought?" Pedro said, "Don't hit it to me."

I know, defensively, early in my career, I'd say, "Don't hit it to me. Hit it to Frank White, our second baseman." I'd think, bring in reliever Dan Quisenberry, who was a right-handed pitcher, because they'd pinch hit a left-handed batter and he'd hit the ball to Frank. As I became more confident defensively I wanted the ball hit to me, and I wound up winning a Gold Glove.

"He was the spokesman on the club his rookie season, and that's a veteran team with a proven ability to win," says Brett. "Not many rookies walk in and find themselves in the spotlight, but he welcomed it."

Chipper showed his ability to rise to the occasion in that four-game series with the New York Mets in September 1999. I'll never forget that series. The Mets were only a game back of the Braves, and Chipper let them know who was in charge. The Braves swept the series and Chipper hit four home runs. He had the best series of the year at the most crucial time of the year. He told the rest of the Braves, "You can rely on me boys. Jump on. We're going to win this thing."

The thing that sticks out about Chipper is he's always been in the spotlight and he has never backed off. He was the spokesman on the club his rookie season, and that's a veteran team with a proven ability to win. Not many rookies walk in and find themselves in the spotlight, but he welcomed it.

He was the No. 1 pick in the country when he came out of high school. He

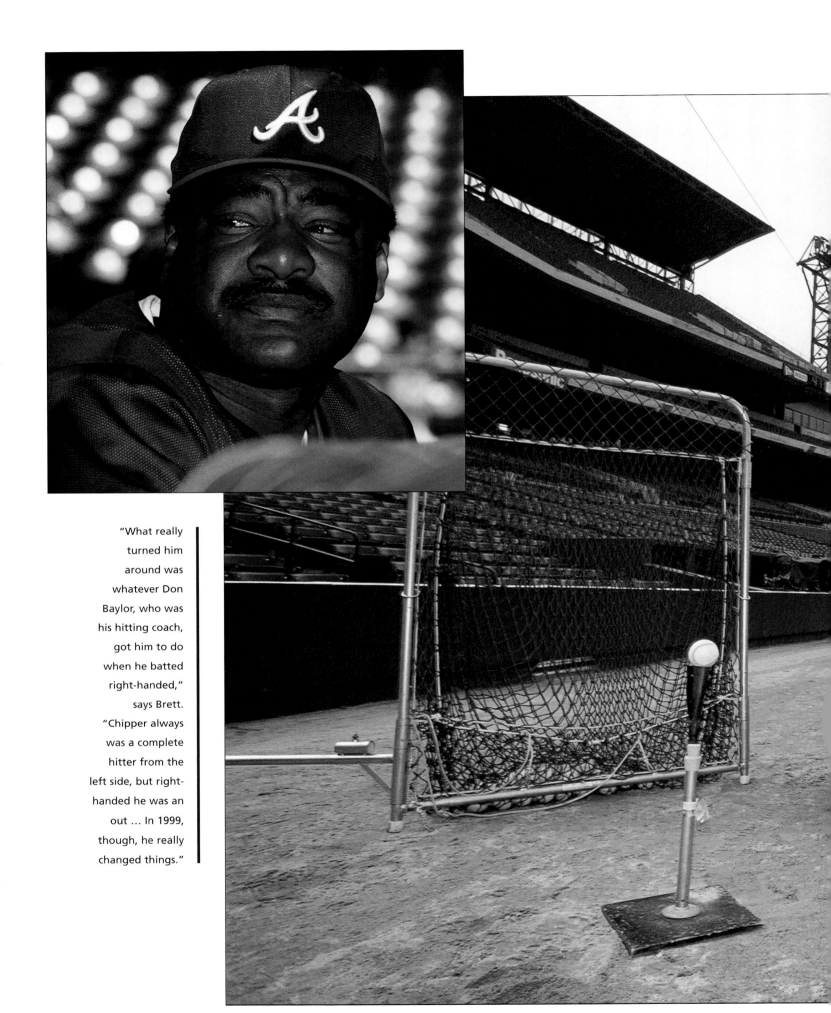

"What really turned him around was whatever Don Baylor, who was his hitting coach, got him to do when he batted right-handed," says Brett. "Chipper always was a complete hitter from the left side, but right-handed he was an out ... In 1999, though, he really changed things."

was in the big leagues at a young age, asked to make the switch from shortstop to third base, and hit third in the order of a team that was the dominant team of the decade. He had success early.

There was a lot of added pressure on him. The way he handled it was because he had a lot of mental confidence. It's more than physical ability. It's the mental toughness. He wants to be the spokesman for the team. He wants the responsibility of being the No. 1 guy on the team.

With that comes some moments that aren't pleasant. After the game, win or lose, the media goes to him. I had to grow into that. I wasn't comfortable with guys always coming to me after games at first. When I came up, I had Hal McRae to handle that post-game pressure. He was the guy we looked to, and then all of a sudden the writers were at my locker. It's something you have to learn to deal with.

And after the 1999 season his stature will only be enhanced.

What really turned him around was whatever Don Baylor, who was his hitting coach, got him to do when he batted right-handed. Chipper always was a

"He showed a lot in 1999 by the way he played despite the people missing in the Atlanta lineup," Brett says. "He proved he could do it on his own."

CHIPPER JONES
CAREER BATTING STATISTICS

Year	Team	Games	At-Bats	Hits	Doubles	Triples	Home Runs	Total Bases	Runs	Runs Batted In	Total Walks	Strikeouts	On-Base Pcnt	Slugging Pcnt	Batting Average
1993	ATL	8	3	2	1	0	0	3	2	0	1	1	.750	1.000	.667
1995	ATL	140	524	139	22	3	23	236	87	7	73	99	.353	.450	.265
1996	ATL	157	598	185	32	5	30	317	114	110	87	88	.393	.530	.309
1997	ATL	157	597	176	41	3	21	286	100	111	76	88	.371	.479	.295
1998	ATL	160	601	188	29	5	34	329	123	107	96	93	.404	.547	.313
1999	ATL	157	567	181	41	1	45	359	116	110	126	94	.441	.633	.319
TOTALS		779	2890	871	166	17	153	1530	542	524	459	463	.394	.529	.301

complete hitter from the left side, but right-handed he was an out. He didn't even scare pitchers with his power potential. In 1999, though, he really changed things.

That's why he went from a great player to an MVP-type player. You can't flip-flop your pitchers anymore figuring you have an advantage against him.

It's a tribute to Don Baylor that he could get his point across, but also a tribute to Chipper that he was willing to listen. He already was a very good player, and when a player reaches that level they don't always listen because they figure they are good enough.

As a hitter you find that one guy you click with and then you build off that. I had Charlie Lau when I was a young player, and struggling. We spent hours together, working on my swing and working on my mental approach.

We'd come out early every day on the road. Sometimes I'd take fifteen swings and he'd say, "Next." Sometimes it would be fifty swings.

It's a maintenance thing. For some reason you can lose it overnight and so you go out and reaffirm what you have to do. You can't do it during regular batting practice when you might get fifteen, twenty swings at the most, have people running the bases and crowds around the batting cage. You need to go out when you can really concentrate on what you're doing.

Don Baylor won't be there for Chipper anymore, but he won't need him. The foundation is there. It's like when Charlie left us in Kansas City. I knew the basics of what I needed to do, and I had Hal McRae and other hitting instructors who knew my swing and could keep me going.

What gets overlooked because of what he does offensively is he is a good defensive player, too. He has the arm strength and range you look for in a third baseman. As he gets more experience and more comfortable he'll be more consistent. It comes with time.

Chipper hopes to stay with the Braves his entire career — much like Brett did with the Royals during his 21-year career.

ADDITIONAL BATTING STATS

Year	Team	Home Runs (Home)	(Road)	Intentional Walks	Hit By Pitch	Sacrifice Hits	Sacrifice Flies
1993	**ATL**	**0**	**0**	**0**	**0**	**0**	**0**
1995	**ATL**	**15**	**8**	**1**	**0**	**1**	**4**
1996	**ATL**	**18**	**12**	**0**	**0**	**1**	**7**
1997	**ATL**	**7**	**14**	**8**	**0**	**0**	**6**
1998	**ATL**	**17**	**17**	**1**	**1**	**1**	**8**
1999	**ATL**	**25**	**20**	**18**	**2**	**0**	**6**
Totals	ATL	82	71	28	3	3	31

But the big thing is his bat. He showed a lot in 1999 by the way he played despite the people missing in the Atlanta lineup. Andres Galarraga was out all season and Javier Lopez was lost midway through the season. Chipper, though, didn't miss a step. He proved he could do it on his own.

the one thing I have noticed the few times I have seen him play is that he smiles a lot.

If you're on the Atlanta Braves you should smile a lot. You know you have a good team. You know you are probably going to win the division. That means you are going to smile a lot in March, April, May, June, July, August and September.

But all of a sudden October comes around and you're not smiling a lot. You are playing teams as good, if not better, and you are getting beat, which you are not used to.

For all the success the Braves had in the '90s — making eight post-season appearances — and they have only one world championship. I know the feeling. We made it into the postseason seven times in ten years [1976–85] and only won one world championship [1985]. Those other years you always wonder what you could have done to make a difference.

But when spring training comes you're smiling again. Chipper has all the reasons in the world to smile and go out and enjoy the game.

He's a great player and making a great living.

"Chipper has all the reasons in the world to smile and go out and enjoy the game," says George Brett.

power on POWER

BY CURT SCHILLING |
AS TOLD TO PAUL HAGEN |

I can still remember the first time I faced Chipper Jones. It was early in the 1995 season, his rookie year, at the old Atlanta-Fulton County Stadium.

In the first inning, I got him on a swinging strikeout. I had a scouting report I thought would work against him. And it did. Since he was a young player, I didn't see any reason to change my approach the next time he came up.

That turned out to be in the third inning. There were runners on first and second with two outs. I decided to stay with the same pitches I had used to strike him out. This time he got a hit — a single to right.

I said to myself, "Wow, that was pretty impressive. Here's a young hitter, but he really made a nice adjustment at the plate. And he made it pretty quickly." You don't see that ability much in guys when they first come up. And I've never forgotten it.

Of course, at the time I already knew the Braves were looking at him as one of their top prospects. I knew that

A true power pitcher, Curt Schilling was the National League strikeout leader in 1997 and 1998.

After striking out swinging in his first at-bat against Curt Schilling, Chipper smacked a single to right field his next time up.

he had been drafted as the first player in the nation a couple years earlier. He was batting third for one of the best teams in baseball. So, naturally, I was going to pay attention.

Still, he made an impression right away, and I've been interested in following his career ever since.

the one thing that strikes you about Chipper right away is that he certainly doesn't lack for confidence. As an opponent, you don't like that. It comes off as cockiness. But that's not a bad thing. A lot of great players have that swagger. You have to have a lot of confidence if you're going to succeed in baseball and Chipper obviously believes in himself. It's just unusual to see a young player have that kind of an aura around him.

Chipper compiled a career year in 1999 with highs in home runs (45), total bases (359), stolen bases (25) and batting average (.319).

It's the kind of quality you love in a guy if he's your teammate, but you don't really care for in somebody on another club.

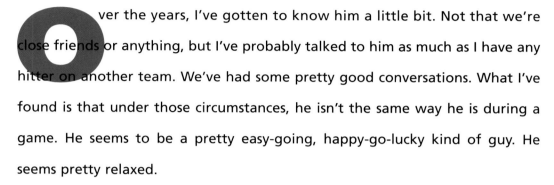

Over the years, I've gotten to know him a little bit. Not that we're close friends or anything, but I've probably talked to him as much as I have any hitter on another team. We've had some pretty good conversations. What I've found is that under those circumstances, he isn't the same way he is during a game. He seems to be a pretty easy-going, happy-go-lucky kind of guy. He seems pretty relaxed.

On the field, he's different. I wasn't surprised to see him voted the Most Valuable Player in 1999. He carried himself like an MVP when he was a rookie. Again, I'm not belittling that. That's a good thing . . . as long as you have the ability to back it up. Which he does.

"He's a fun guy to play with and a fun guy to have on your team," says Braves pitcher John Rocker. "But I know I'd hate to have to face him."

As a pitcher you have to get through that mystique. He's hit me pretty well at times, but I'm going to go out there and challenge him. I feel like I can beat him every time he comes up. And I know he feels he like he can get the best of me every time. That's what makes facing him a lot of fun as well as a heck of a challenge.

There are a lot of good hitters in the major leagues. I think what sets Chipper apart, what makes him special, is that he has that rare ability to be at his best in the clutch. That's something the great players can do.

He's one of the few guys who seems to be even better in the late innings, with runners in scoring position, in games that count the most. He's definitely one of those hitters a pitcher doesn't want to see coming to the plate when the game is on the line.

A three-time All-Star, Curt Schilling has a career 3.38 ERA, and his strikeouts per nine innings (8.36) is in the top ten among active pitchers.

"What makes him so tough is that he can hit anyone's fastball," Schilling says. "I'm a power pitcher but with Chipper you have to mix it up and use both sides of the plate a little more than you would with most guys."

A lot of teams tend to pitch around him. Not that the Braves don't have other good hitters, but you can see why some teams would try that. So it's a testament to him that he was able to put up the numbers he has when he doesn't always get a pitch to hit. I guess when you're that talented, you can do that.

He's hit three or four homers off me. I remember one in particular. He hit it out to dead center. The thing that was most impressive was that, off the bat, I didn't think he had hit it that well. And it still went out in the deepest part of the park. So you know how strong he is.

What makes him so tough is that he can hit anyone's fastball. I'm a power pitcher but with Chipper you have to mix it up and use both sides of the plate a little more than you would with most guys.

I might throw more curves, sliders and splitters than usual. I might try to make the fastball almost a surprise. Or maybe pound him inside with fastballs early in the count and then try to come back and get him out with something soft on the outside.

Or you could try staying with the fastball but mixing up the location. Really, that's what makes him so good. There's not one way you can pitch him to be successful. As soon as you think you've got something figured out, as I said, he has the ability to make an adjustment.

Schilling still remembers a home run Chipper hit off him to dead center field. "The thing that was most impressive was that, off the bat, I didn't think he had hit it that well."

"I feel like I can beat him every time he comes up," says Schilling. "And I know he feels like he can get the best of me every time."

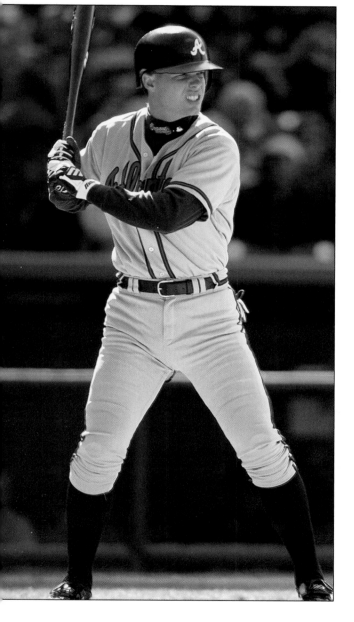

Schilling has seen definite improvement in Chipper's right-handed swing. "Now he can definitely hurt you from both sides of the plate."

I don't think Chipper has changed much since he first came up. He was a pretty complete player from the beginning. Even as a rookie, he didn't have too many holes in his game.

What's really impressive is how consistent he's been over the years. He plays almost every day. You can count on him to hit his thirty homers and drive in his one hundred runs. And everybody knows how important consistency is in baseball.

If there's one difference, it's that he's really stepped up and become a much better right-handed hitter. Earlier in his career, you could almost pitch around him by bringing in a left-handed reliever to face him. He didn't have nearly the power when he batted right-handed.

That's not the case anymore. Now he can definitely hurt you from both sides of the plate. That's probably the biggest difference I see.

I guess that's why he had kind of a breakthrough season. But I can't say I was surprised. He's one of the best hitters and all-around players in the league. I could see that he had a chance to be something special the first game I pitched against him.

the Hot corner

BY DARRELL EVANS
AS TOLD TO DAN SCHLOSSBERG

Darrell Evans hit 414 home runs during a twenty-one-year career that started with the 1969 Atlanta Braves. The two-time All-Star had his best year in 1973, when he joined Hank Aaron and Davey Johnson as the first trio of teammates to hit forty home runs in the same season.

Playing third base was a lot of fun. It's one of those positions where you have a chance to make a spectacular play every game. That's what you do when you're at the top level — you look to make those kinds of plays. The routine ones aren't as exciting.

At third base, you can get the slow roller, the tough backhand, the in-between hop, or a ball that makes you dive to your left. I loved playing third base, and the Braves over the years have had nothing but great third basemen.

I was very fortunate to grow up being a left-handed hitter who played third base, just like Eddie Mathews, the Hall of Famer who spent most of his career with the Braves. Eddie was the hitting coach and then became the manager after I got to the Braves. I couldn't have had a better teacher.

He was exactly the way I thought he was going to be: a tough guy who worked me particularly hard. I was really fortunate to have such a great teacher. And I took No. 41

in his honor after I left the Braves. [It was retired in Atlanta].

After I left, Bob Horner played third in Atlanta and Terry Pendleton won a batting title and MVP award while leading the worst-to-first team of 1991. Then Chipper Jones came along and won his own MVP while playing the same position.

Chipper has added his name to the impressive roster of All-Star third basemen for the Braves. Bob Elliott, Eddie Mathews, Darrell Evans, Bob Horner and Terry Pendelton have fifteen All-Star selections between them while playing for the Braves.

I feel real good about being one of those guys who played third for the Braves.

The position isn't easy. I know Chipper had only eleven games during [a strike-shortened] spring training to make the transition from shortstop to third base. It's a lot harder than people realize.

At shortstop, you get to read the hops a little more. Of course, you have to cover a bit more ground too. At third, a lot of times you just knock the ball down or let it hit off your chest. Then you can throw guys out if you have a pretty strong arm.

Chipper's a great athlete, I think that's a big part of it. He's a great adjuster. Third base requires more quickness than speed. Brooks Robinson and Graig Nettles weren't known for their speed but they had quick reactions. When you have a great athlete like Chipper, that helps.

Attitude has a lot to do it with it. A lot of guys just don't want to move from short to third. You grew up

"Chipper's a great athlete, I think that's a big part of it," Evans says. "He's a great adjuster. Third base requires more quickness than speed."

"We know what kind of offensive player he is," says Evans. "Defensively, he's a good one too."

"It looks like he has a lot of fun playing the game," says Evans. "He's the kind of guy everybody looks to as a leader."

playing shortstop, where everybody puts the best player, and, all of a sudden, you could take it as being a failure and not put the time in. Obviously, that's not what happened with Chipper. He was just the opposite.

He went out there and tried to make himself as good as he could be. We know what kind of offensive player he is. Defensively, he's a good one too.

Chipper is a tough-nosed kid. That's what you look for. Guys who have played a long time always ask themselves, "How does he go about playing a ballgame?"

Chipper is always in the middle of everything. He's either making a big play or driving in a big run. Plus he has presence. A lot is probably not said about how certain guys affect the lineup.

| CAREER FIELDING STATISTICS

Year	Team	Position	Games	Games Started	Total Chances	Put Outs	Assists	Errors	Double Plays	Fielding Percentage
1993	ATL	SS	3	0	2	1	1	0	0	1.000
1995	ATL	3B	123	121	360	81	254	25	19	.931
1995	ATL	OF	20	17	23	22	1	0	0	1.000
1996	ATL	3B	118	116	246	48	185	13	9	.947
1996	ATL	SS	38	38	160	53	103	4	27	.975
1996	ATL	OF	1	1	2	2	0	0	0	1.000
1997	ATL	3B	152	151	333	77	241	15	17	.955
1997	ATL	OF	5	3	6	6	0	0	0	1.000
1998	ATL	3B	158	158	407	105	290	12	28	.971
1999	ATL	3B	156	156	343	88	238	17	10	.950
1999	ATL	SS	1	0	1	0	1	0	0	1.000
Totals			766	761	1883	483	1314	86	110	.954

"Chipper is always in the middle of everything," Evans says. "He's either making a big play or driving in a big run."

For one thing, Chipper is a switch-hitter. He came on to be a superstar on the right side last year. That made it really tough for the pitchers, since it made everybody around him better.

You've got to give the guy credit: With Andres Galarraga out last year, he didn't have the lineup protection he had before. I can't say enough about him. It's fun to watch him play. It looks like he has a lot of fun playing the game. He's the kind of guy everybody looks to as a leader. He deserves what he got [the MVP]. When you have those kinds of statistics, you're a feared hitter in every kind of way.

When you become an MVP, people are saying you're as good as anybody in the game. I don't get to see him on a everyday basis so I think there are other guys in that category, but what other third baseman can you name that you'd like to start a ballclub with? As I said, you've got to be a tough-nosed guy, so certainly he's got to be on that team somewhere.

Last year, Chipper broke Todd Hundley's record for home runs by a National League switch-hitter. I think he could go after Mickey Mantle's

From Sammy Sosa to Kenny Rogers, Jones is a magnet for celebrities both inside and outside the sport of baseball.

Evans says that he thinks Chipper has a good chance to break Mickey Mantle's major-league season record for home runs by a switch-hitter [fifty-four].

"It will be fun to see how he progresses,
says Evans. "It looks like there's
no ceiling for him."

major-league record of fifty-four. The way guys hit the ball now, that's certainly within reach.

As a player, you mature and start to figure out what the situation dictates. Chipper's not only a slugger but a .300 hitter. I never hit for that kind of average and knew I probably wasn't going to. I had to use my power a little more. In certain situations, you have to look to hit home runs.

So many factors enter into it. Fifty home runs is still an awful lot of home runs; it just doesn't happen all the time.

You have to have that kind of year where you're healthy and you can get in those big streaks. Chipper certainly looks like he's capable, because the right-handed stroke came along last year. He had done everything almost exclusively left-handed. All of a sudden, people had to stop turning him around like they did before. That gave him more opportunities.

It will be fun to see how he progresses. It looks like there's no ceiling for him.

One of the things Eddie Mathews taught me was to give back to the game. I had so many people help me: Mickey Vernon was my Triple-A manager and [Hall of Famer] Luke Appling helped with my hitting. There were so many people who helped me and now I'm trying to give something back. As a manager or coach, you can do that.

I think Chipper is the kind of guy who also will stay in the game after his playing days. He knows so much about the game that he could share with young players. But that day is a long way off.

CHAPTER 8

chemistry 101

BY TOM GLAVINE
AS TOLD TO DAN SCHLOSSBERG

i first saw Chipper Jones during spring training in 1994. He was in camp as an outfielder because that was the year our leftfielder, Ronnie Gant, got hurt [fractured leg in a dirt-bike accident]. Chipper was such a good athlete that you would have sworn he'd played the outfield his whole career.

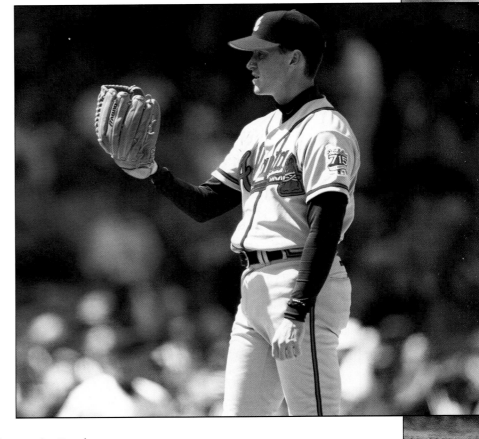

You could tell right away that he could play. All of us had heard the reports on him: what a good athlete he was, how he was a "can't-miss" prospect. I think you hear that so much that you don't pay a lot of attention to it. But he was one of the few guys who actually lived up to his billing and was an impressive talent right from the get-go.

Tom Glavine has won two National League Cy Young awards and a World Series MVP trophy during his thirteen-year career with the Atlanta Braves. He's the only major league pitcher to post four twenty-win seasons during the 1990s.

Glavine says that Chipper leads more by example than by words. "Certainly when you're going out there and putting up the numbers Chipper is putting up, you lead by example."

Tom Glavine considers Chipper and Andres Galarraga as the Braves team leaders in the infield.

I really wasn't sure he could be a big-league shortstop. I knew he had played there in the minor leagues but had also heard he had trouble there — particularly with his throwing. It was kind of a wait-and-see thing if he would make the club as an outfielder but unfortunately he hurt his knee and missed the season.

When he came back in 1995, spring training was shortened to eleven exhibition games because of the strike. We needed a third base-man, so they moved him there.

Because he was accustomed to shortstop, playing another position on the infield was a little easier transition than if he had come from the outfield to third base.

Everybody felt moving him to third would eliminate a lot of his errors but he'd have to make more "reaction" plays than he did at shortstop. It's a little more difficult to play short than it is to play third, but there was no question he had to learn a new position and learn it at the big-league level. That wasn't an easy thing to do.

he's improved a lot. He's worked at it and gotten better as a result. Chipper makes virtually all the plays over there now. He still has some lapses, as we all do, but for a guy who hasn't been playing the position very long, he fields very well. I wouldn't be surprised if sometime in the near future he's not a Gold Glove third baseman.

Chipper would have to be considered the leader of the infield, though a healthy Andres Galarraga would assume a lot of leadership roles simply because of who he is and the respect level he carries with the players.

Chipper's one of our leaders because we expect a lot of production out of him.

Anytime you have that kind of pressure on you to produce, along with it comes responsibility as a leader. But that's one of the great things about our team — we've always had a number of guys we consider leaders. And it's always been helpful for us to have that many leader-type guys, and helpful for the young guys to have guys to look up to.

I was very fortunate to play with both [two-time MVP] Dale Murphy and Chipper Jones. And I think there's a comparison between the two of them. Certainly, their fan following is similar. I think Chipper has that All-American look about him that people like. That's obviously one of the traits Dale had.

All of us have a long way to go to get to Dale's stature in terms of what he did, how he conducted himself, and what he did for his community. I don't know that anybody will ever really reach the levels Dale Murphy reached. But it's a compliment to Chipper to be mentioned in the same vein as Dale. He's got a way to go but he's certainly on the right track.

Like Dale, Chipper is pretty quiet in the clubhouse. He doesn't say a whole lot. He spends a lot of time playing cards and doing that kind of stuff. He's more of a leader by example than he is vocally. I don't think we have the kind of club that needs a lot of that. Certainly when you're going out there and putting up the numbers Chipper is putting up, you lead by example.

In my mind, that's the best way to do things. I'm not so interested all the time in what you have to say — I want to see what you're doing, day in and day out, when you think people aren't looking. Day in and day out, Chipper works pretty hard at what he does and it's made him a better player.

"I'd pitch Chipper the same way I'd pitch a Larry Walker, Sammy Sosa, or Mark McGwire," Glavine says. "You have to understand that if you make mistakes, they're going to make you pay."

Chipper Jones nearly single-handedly beat the Yankees with this fourth-inning home run off of Orlando Hernandez in Game One of the 1999 World Series. The Yankees came back with four runs in the eighth inning to win the game, 4–1.

He has definitely matured as a player. He's gotten consistently better, both offensively and defensively. In 1999, he had a career year and came through as the National League's Most Valuable Player. That shows his maturation on the field.

Off the field, he's been through some tough things personally that have forced him to grow up, so to speak. He's handled those situations fairly well. He stood up to them, admitted his mistakes, and was up-front with people. That shows a level of maturity some guys don't have.

All across the board, he's grown up a little bit and matured a little bit, and I'm sure he'll continue to do so even more in the future.

I'll tell you one thing about Chipper Jones: When I first saw him, I didn't think he'd hit forty-five home runs a year. But there are a lot of guys in the league I couldn't imagine hitting the amount of home runs they are hitting now.

"I enjoy having Chipper as a teammate," says Glavine. "He's a great player and great players ultimately make guys like myself better and our team better."

When you first saw Chipper, you saw a guy who could hit for average, hit for power, and drive guys in. When he first came up — which wasn't very long ago — thirty runs and one hundred runs batted in were marks of a guy who was viewed as a good player. Chipper was looked at as that kind of guy. It's just that the bar has been raised a little bit and now thirty home runs and one hundred RBI aren't so great anymore.

But Chipper has made the leap to the next level of forty home runs and 120-plus RBI, along with some other guys.

I know Don Baylor had some tips that Chipper took advantage of last year — especially when batting right-handed — but a lot of his success came from Chipper himself. You can get all the coaching you want but you have to go out there, utilize the teachings, and make it work for you. Chipper had to trust the ideas and make them work. Obviously, he did that.

If we weren't teammates, the way I would pitch to Chipper would depend upon the situation. With all good hitters, you have to maintain a level of aggressiveness but at the same time be careful. You pitch guys a lot differently with two outs and nobody on than you do with the tying run in scoring position.

I'd pitch Chipper the same way I'd pitch a Larry Walker, Sammy Sosa, or Mark McGwire. You have to understand that if you make mistakes, they're going to make you pay.

As an opposing pitcher, Chipper would be the guy I'd look at and say, "I'm not going to let this guy beat me." I would do everything I could not to let him come up in a situation where he could hurt me.

Despite Chipper's disregard for his body on the field, he hasn't missed any significant playing time from injury since his ACL tear in 1993.

Look what he did down the stretch in 1999: he was on fire, particularly in the home-and-home series we had with the Mets late in the season. That went a long way toward winning him the MVP award. People remember an awful lot about how you finish, and Chipper finished as hot as anybody.

I don't think his total of forty-five home runs last year is going to be his career high; I think he can do better than that. We'll have to see whether he can hit ten more to break Mickey Mantle's major-league record for home runs by a switch-hitter [fifty-four in 1961]. I certainly think he has the potential to do it.

The nature of baseball is changing so much. Who would've thought anybody would break Roger Maris' record? Now it's been broken by nine home runs. Mantle's mark is certainly attainable, especially if Chipper continues to progress the way he has based upon last season.

Both Chipper and Glavine were named to the 1997 All-Star Game, along with teammates, Jeff Blauser, Denny Neagle, Greg Maddux, Javier Lopez and the Braves coaching staff. Kenny Lofton made the team but was injured and didn't play.

I think Chipper is a great hitter — there's no doubt about that — but I think he's more likely to win a Gold Glove trophy than a batting crown. It's awfully difficult for guys to hit for power like he does and win a batting title. It seems like you've got to make up your mind to be one or the other.

Chipper is going to be counted on in our lineup as a guy who's going to produce runs and hit home runs. When you're that kind of hitter, you tend to extend your strike zone from time to time because you're the guy who needs to drive in runs. So winning a batting title would be difficult for him but not out of the question.

I enjoy having Chipper as a teammate. He's a great player and great players ultimately make guys like myself better and our team better.

I would much rather have Chipper on my team than to be playing against him. It's fun being able to sit back and watch a guy's career progress.

First it was Chipper Jones, the guy with all the potential. How much of it was he going to fulfill? Now it's Chipper Jones, the MVP. He's certainly gotten better over his career and I'm sure he's going to continue to get better.

That's fun to watch and it makes all of us better.

Bob Costas says that Chipper Jones has a "throwback appeal" and looks like a ballplayer. Chipper would fit right in on this 1956 Topps Mickey Mantle baseball card.

MICKEY MANTLE
outfield NEW YORK YANKEES

the Throwback

BY BOB COSTAS
AS TOLD TO JOHN DELCOS

With NBC since 1980, Bob Costas is considered a premier baseball broadcaster and analyst. He has hosted nearly every major sporting event, including numerous World Series, Super Bowls, NBA Championships and Olympics.

Chipper Jones has a different kind of appeal. Part of Chipper's appeal, and I've thought this from the first time I saw him in 1995 as a big leaguer, is that he looks like a guy off a baseball card in 1955 — especially with the close-cropped hair.

He looks like a kid. He actually bears some facial resemblance to Gil McDougald, who used to play for the Yankees — although people talk about him as the young Mantle because he's a switch-hitter. He does have a throwback appeal in that respect. And, he has a name — Chipper Jones — that sounds like it's out of a Chip Hilton sports book or a Gill Thorpe comic strip: Chipper Jones ... switch-hitter ... very good ball player. He just looks like he's a ball-player.

I think a lot of Chipper's appeal comes from the SuperStation TBS, because they are always on television. The Braves, although they've been disappointing in the post-season, they are always there, so they are always playing in big games. Because of that, people see him a lot and know about him.

Chipper has a likable quality about him. What most people see is a kid out of a Norman Rockwell painting playing baseball. He just looks like a ballplayer ... he gets his uniform dirty.

But, people aren't completely naïve. Chipper had his own fairly well publicized personal problems. But, people forget those things. Unless it's a major thing that the media covers relentlessly, I think that stuff kind of goes into the background fairly quickly. Chipper, himself, has taken responsibility. He's acknowledged his mistakes and tried to do the right thing, subsequently.

As great as the Yankees are as a team, the only player on their team — with the exception of Roger Clemens — who I would confidently predict will be a Hall of Famer is Derek Jeter. I think it's less certain, but very possible, Jones could also be a Hall of Fame player.

With a shortstop with numbers like Jeter's, barring injury and he keeps doing what he's established, he can't miss making the Hall of Fame. I think there's a little more doubt with Chipper. Not much, but a little more doubt.

He had a very strong September, and played well against the Mets. That definitely enhanced his image as a money player, an impact player.

"He just looks like a ballplayer... he gets his uniform dirty," says Bob Costas.

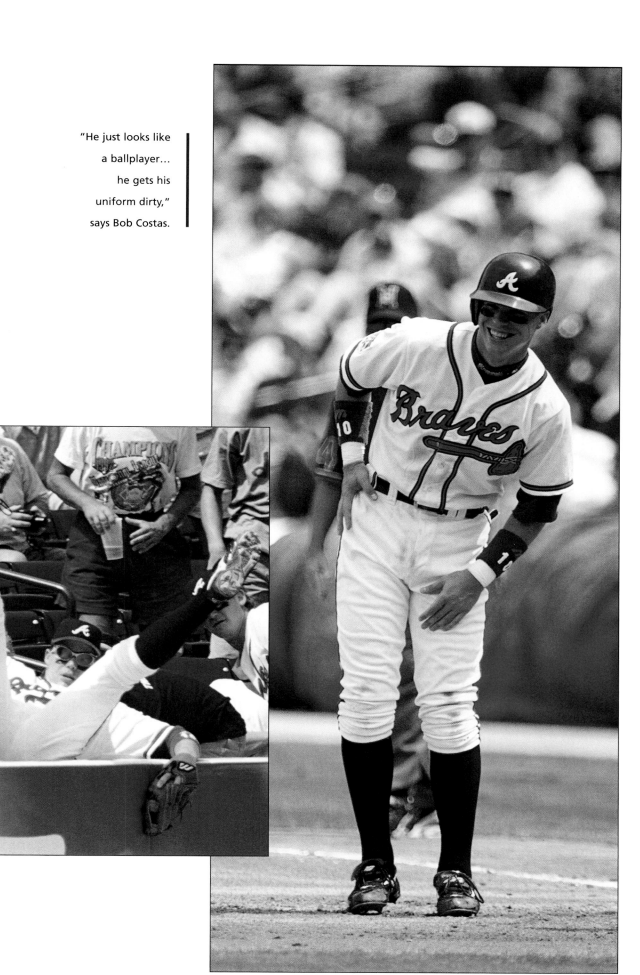

EDITORIAL CREDITS

John Delcos, who interviewed Bob Costas, covers the New York Yankees and Major League Baseball for the Gannett Journal News in Westchester, NY.

Paul Hagen, who interviewed Curt Schilling, has covered baseball for twenty-five years for the Dallas Times Herald, Fort Worth Star-Telegram and Philadelphia Daily News.

Bob Nightengale, who interviewed Tony Gwynn, is the National Baseball columnist for USA Today's Baseball Weekly. He has been a long-time beat writer covering baseball for the Kansas City Times-Star and the Los Angeles Times. Nightengale, a 1979 graduate of Arizona State University, was the beat writer for the Kansas City Royals, San Diego Padres, Anaheim Angels and Los Angeles Dodgers.

Marty Noble, who wrote the "Heart of the Braves" chapter, is a reporter for Newsday. He's covered the National League, the Mets, Chipper Jones and their rivalries since Chipper's been in the league.

Tracy Ringolsby, who interviewed George Brett, is covering his twenty-fifth season of Major League Baseball. He is a baseball writer for the Denver Rocky Mountain News and one of the originators of Baseball America.

Dan Schlossberg, who interviewed Hank Aaron, Bobby Cox, Larry Jones Sr., Darrell Evans and Tom Glavine, is baseball editor of The Encyclopedia Americana Annual and the author of twenty-one books, including The Baseball Catalog, Millennium Edition (Jonathan David Publishers), available this spring from www.amazon.com.

PHOTO CREDITS

All photography by Tom DiPace unless otherwise noted.

AP/Wide World Photos: 32(top left)
John Cordes/Allsport: 99
Scott Cunningham: 6–7, 29, 32, 73, 110
Mike Dehoog/TDP: 67(left), 74(top right)
David Durochik: 16, 70(right)
Stephen Green/Major League Baseball: 101
Chris Hamilton: 8, 24, 25, 51, 69, 77, 83, 87, 90, 91, 100(top), 103, 106–107
Courtesy of Lynn Jones: 18(top left), 19, 43, 44, 45, 48, 49, 52, 53, 54, 55, 56, 57
Allen Kee/BRSP: 75
John Klein/Major League Baseball: 86
Jim McLean: 11, 63, 72
Rich Pilling/Major League Baseball: 74
Profile/Major League Baseball: 9(top)
Sports Imagery: 60(bottom)
Courtesy of Stetson University: 47, 54-55
Rob Tringali/SportsChrome: 23, 81, 100(bottom)
Ron Vesely: 9(bottom), 21(left), 31, 40, 59, 61, 76, 89, 104–105, 109
Michael Zito/SportsChrome: 66, 67(right), 108(top)
Joel Zwink/Major League Baseball: 58